CRIMES WITHOUT PUNISHMENT
CICIG IMPUNITY IN GUATEMALA

Liga Pro Patria
Guatemala 2021
ISBN: 9798494798459

All rights reserved.

CICIG AND THE RULE OF LAW
Table of Contents

FOREWORD

The International Commission Against Impunity in Guatemala (CICIG), the foreign entity at the heart of Guatemala's political and legal system, is actually near its closely-held goal of establishing itself as the director of Guatemala's destiny. These reports are meant to open the curtain and let things be seen.

Part 1
Murder by Diplomatic Immunity

A police force directed by the CICIG and its handmaiden, Guatemala's Justice Ministry (MP), makes an illegal pre-dawn raid against a residence in the capital city and kills the wrong man. In response to a lawsuit, the CICIG invokes diplomatic immunity, absolving itself; while the MP says no crime occurred.

Part 2
The President Versus the Commissioner

Guatemala's President Morales, as part of his power to expel any diplomat, orders the CICIG commissioner, Iván Velásquez, to leave the country. In violation of national and international law, Guatemala's high court reverses the president's order and puts Velásquez above any justice.

CRIMES WITHOUT PUNSHIMENT

Part 3
From Here to Eternity: The Pavón Prison Cases

In 2006, Guatemalan forces re-established order in the country's toughest prison. The country's human-rights ombudsman – who at first praised the operation, in which seven inmates died – later asked the CICIG to prosecute. The result is a travesty that violates the norms of justice and continues to this day.

Part 4
The Case of the Disappearing Attorney General

Working with Guatemala's president, its high court, and the US ambassador, the CICIG engineers a judicial coup that removes Attorney General Conrado Reyes from office. This 2010 coup marks the first of the CICIG's efforts to remake the country's political and legal system in its own image.

Part 5
Soviet Show-Trials in the Americas: The Case of the CICIG versus Moisés Galindo

With the help of Guatemala's justice ministry and judges, the CICIG goes after Moisés Galindo, an attorney who has opposed the commission in court. The CICIG breaks a lawful bond between the attorney and his client, imprisons Galindo, confiscates his property, and prosecutes against the rules.

Part 6
Seven Years in Prison for Nothing at All

In an effort to give cover to Guatemala's besieged president, the CICIG injects itself into a prominent murder case far beyond its mandate. As a result of testimony coerced by the CICIG, two brothers spend seven years in jail before a judge finally frees them, declaring that the CICIG has not made a case.

TABLE OF CONTENTS

Part 7
The CICIG in Brief: or, Progressives Against the Fools' Brigade

A short history of the controversial commission shows that Guatemala's leaders didn't want the CICIG, perceiving it to be at odds with the country's sovereignty and laws. Even so, the country bowed to international pressure and welcomed the CICIG – a decision that Guatemalans today increasingly regret.

Part 8
The CICIG and Guatemala's Constitution

The CICIG sponsors an effort to rewrite Guatemala's Constitution, with the evident goal of bringing radical change to the country's laws. The CICIG is violating the law in doing so. The justice minister attacks Congress's right to free speech, while the US removes a congressman's visa for US travel.

Part 9
The Lawlessness of Guatemala's Justice

CICIG commissioner Velásquez and Justice Minister Aldana press their attacks against Congressman Fernando Linares, who has vigorously opposed their project for radical changes to the Constitution. The US embassy piles on Linares, thereby involving the US in an effort that undermines law and liberty.

Part 10
Imperialism in Latin America

The Obama administration announced the end of US imperialism. But imperialism has only changed form. It is now being delivered by institutions from inside Guatemala; notably by the country's high court and especially by the CICIG, which is promoting a radical takeover with help from the US.

Part 11
"Open, Sesame!" The Triumph of Politics Over Justice

The CICIG is consolidating its control over judicial appointments as a means to control what is law and what is not. A feature of this takeover is the language now being used to express legal concepts; its relationship to law is no greater than that of the magical phrase written for Ali Baba and his 40 thieves.

CONCLUSION
The Runaway Commission

The CICIG came to Guatemala to oversee the dismantling of subversive groups that were robbing the people of their liberties. Instead, the CICIG has itself become the leading subversive entity. It's time for the CICIG to submit to oversight, and for Guatemalans to reclaim their sovereignty and laws.

AFTERWORD
The Ministry of Virtue

A renowned academician and commentator, Armando de la Torre has been opposing the CICIG ever since it was publicly proposed. Unlike some others, Dr. de la Torre does not see the CICIG as a good idea gone bad. He sees it as a bad idea that has fulfilled its destiny.

FOREWORD

The International Commission Against Impunity in Guatemala (CICIG) is the predominant and most powerful institution in Guatemala. It has generated plenty of coverage – but only in the superficial mode of present-day journalism.

Reporters have taken the commission largely at its word, while scrutiny has gone missing. The purpose behind the following series of narratives is to open the way to scrutiny.

Ever since the beginning of its charmed career, the CICIG – acronym pronounced «see-SEEG» – has been awash in buzzwords. In describing itself and its mission, the CICIG has invariably used terms like anti-impunity, anti-corruption, pro-human rights, pro-indigenous rights, pro-women's rights, and others of the kind. These also happen to be the buzzwords of an international political movement which identifies itself as "progressive" and which regards the CICIG as a crucial component.

In the narratives that follow, we will not judge the labels that the CICIG has affixed to itself; nor will we propose other labels. We will simply recount a series of legal or law-enforcement situations in which the CICIG has chosen to involve itself. To provide contrast, we will describe at least one situation in which the CICIG chose not to involve itself.

These narratives are aimed at policymakers, at journalists, at students, and at the interested general reader. With subjects chosen by legal experts, they are based on court documents, on direct or primary sources, and on news reports.

CRIMES WITHOUT PUNSHIMENT

Our aim is not one of 'exposing' the CICIG in a journalistic sense. It is, rather, to draw the curtain aside and let the reader form his or her own impressions. These pieces are not scholarly works, nor are they lawyer's treatises. Across the various episodes, a coherent picture does take shape, which readers may discover at their own pace.

We do not hope or pretend that our portrayals will be to everybody's liking. The field that these narratives treat is a highly charged and politicized one, with issues that touch on life and death. Our writing on these matters is also an invitation to a dialogue about them. Our aim, rather than controversy, is to raise curiosity. We don't demand to be taken at our word, as others in this field sometimes do. If we inspire readers to explore the issues on their own, our highest goal will have been attained.

CIGIG and the Rule of Law: A report
PROLOGUE

A little more than three years ago, the Liga Pro Patria together with three other civic organizations published the following investigative report, CIGIG and the Rule of Law, about the activities of the International Commission Against Impunity in Guatemala. Like any document worthy of the name, the report was scrupulously researched, carefully prepared, and based on the factual record.

By the spring of 2018, the CICIG was the most powerful political player in Guatemala. Its position put it at odds with its own mandate, which was to help the Ministry of Justice break up illegal entities that threatened Guatemala's liberty. During the prior decade, the CICIG had become the very kind of force it had pledged to eradicate. It was swallowing the freedoms of Guatemalans and was trying to turn the country into a new kind of totalitarian state.

Shortly after we published our report, a striking series of developments put a stop to the CICIG's power-grab. Almost at once, the commission fell into a well-deserved disgrace. While we can't claim a role in that process, our report had pointed to the new trajectory. A few months later, President Jimmy Morales informed Secretary General of the United Nations Antonio Guterres that he would not allow CICIG commissioner Ivan Velázquez to return to Guatemala. Morales requested Guterres name a new commissioner. Commissioner Iván Velázquez, a Colombian aligned with the narcoterrorist group FARC according to Judicial Watch, had been a snake's head in human form. Without him, the CICIG was all but boarded up. In violation of international law, Guterres did not send a replacement and worked to reinsert Velázquez. Responding to this and further CICIG skullduggery, Morales in January 2019 took a step he and his predecessors had been afraid to try. In full accord with international law and precedent, Morales ended the CICIG in Guatemala.

Today, Velázquez and his friends have new cause for hope.

During its rise to power, the CICIG enjoyed the patronage of Barack Obama and Joe Biden. As Obama's emissary, Biden trampled on Guatemalan president Otto Pérez for suggesting that Guatemalans might prefer to see the commission gone. Pérez was deposed from office and jailed by the CICIG on corruption charges that are still untested in court. As of this writing, Pérez's attorney is also in jail, caught in a CICIG sting that our report describes in detail.

Biden, his fellow Democrats, and the State Department know they will be unable to impose another Cicig. They have opted to unilaterally create what they call a working group for the northern triangle. Such an entity cannot work legally in Guatemala because our country has not given and will not give its consent. It would violate the law and set a bad precedent for neighboring nations. Our report, CIGIG and the Rule of Law, has never been more relevant or urgent than it is today.

PART 1:
MURDER BY DIPLOMATIC IMMUNITY

In October 2016, a squad of officers under orders of the UN "anti-corruption commission" and its handmaiden, Guatemala's justice ministry, raided a private residence in order to carry out an arrest-and-search in a case of suspected money laundering.

The UN commission, known by its Spanish acronym CICIG, had gained its charter a decade earlier to work with Guatemala's justice ministry (MP) in eradicating extra-legal, clandestine organizations that might threaten democratic and civic freedoms. In its ten years – as this case and numerous others show – the CICIG has strayed far from its founding mission.

In this raid upon a private residence, the threat to freedom actually came from the pretended remedy – the CICIG's own activity – which bids fair to be called murder by diplomatic immunity.

The facts

On October 28, 2016, armed officers of the CICIG and the MP executed an arrest-and-search warrant at a residence in a gated community of the capital city. The target was a certain Ronald Giovanni García Navarijo, one of seven suspects in a banking fraud and money-laundering scheme.

Well before 6 a.m., armed officers took control of the gated community in which the target residence was located. By law, all residences are inviolable between 6 p.m. and 6 a.m.; so that when armed officers burst into the home, they were sensibly presumed to be criminals and not law-enforcement officers.

Someone inside the home, sensibly enough, took up a defensive posture. A gun battle ensued, and the occupant was killed. Twitter published reports of the shooting at 5:40 and 5:42 a.m., time-stamps that proved unlawful entry.

The major illegality was that officers had killed the wrong man. The deceased was not the subject of the warrant at all; he was Pavel Centeno, an attorney and former Guatemalan finance minister.

The legal process

Five days later, November 2, the Foundation Against Terrorism in Guatemala, a nonprofit group, filed a criminal complaint against CICIG commissioner Iván Velásquez, as well as against MP personnel involved in the botched operation.

A court ordered the MP to investigate. Three weeks later, on November 22, the MP moved to quash the order on grounds that Velásquez and the CICIG could not be charged because they were protected by diplomatic immunity.

The CICIG likewise refused the summons, pointing to the Vienna Convention on Diplomatic Immunity and saying the matter could only be raised in diplomatic channels.

On November 23 the court agreed with the CICIG and the MP; it freed Velásquez and other CICIG personnel from judgment in the case.

Regarding Centeno himself, the MP ruled his death a suicide and moved to dismiss the matter – effectively saying that no crime had occurred.

Apart from the MP's obvious interest in squelching the matter, its claim was shot full of holes, as it were, by the National Institute of Forensic Sciences, which reported that two bullets had entered the

dead man's body; one in the right arm, the other in the head.
Photos of the cadaver showed Centeno's left hand holding a bullet clip. That gave him no means to shoot himself in the head – while casings from police-caliber weapons were found all over the scene.
A year after the shooting, October 31, 2017, the Foundation Against Terrorism was notified that the court had scheduled a hearing for November 15 to consider its complaint against the MP. This hearing was subsequently postponed to early 2018.

Observations

The MP had a legal obligation to know who was actually living at the home it had targeted with its warrant. As late as the moment at which the strike force took control of the community gate, it could have established that the subject of the warrant did not live in the residence; and that Pavel Centeno was the actual occupant.

According to reports, Centeno's wife Nathalie Devaux said the officers detained her and her children for several hours without identifying themselves, and without explaining why they had occupied her home by force of arms.

Together with the illegal timing of the raid, the failure of law-enforcement officers to identify themselves would explain why Centeno resisted; he simply presumed that the attackers were criminals.

Legal Analysis

From publicly available information, it is not possible to determine with certainty how Centeno died. But numerous elements point to an official cover-up and denial of a crime.

The facts of the case could still lead to criminal charges against ministry personnel. The circumstances require the justice minister to name a special prosecutor, but the minister has not done so.

Even if one were to accept the claim of suicide, there remain serious errors by the authorities that would warrant a special prosecutor. Some of those are: faulty intelligence regarding the subject of the warrant; assaulting a residence at an hour prohibited by law; officers not properly identifying themselves before invading the residence; and shell-casings of police- caliber weapons which indicate that the victim was fired upon by the invading officers.

Conclusions

The proverbial gorilla-in-the-room is the unauthorized, unethical and lethal participation of the UN commission in an event that has the look of state-sanctioned murder.

While justice ministry personnel are subject to investigation and prosecution, CICIG personnel are free of those restraints due to their diplomatic immunity. Even so – or especially so – the CICIG's involvement in this case raises questions that cry out for independent evaluation.

As matters now stand, no one can deprive the CICIG of its main weapon: the blanket diplomatic immunity in which the commission's members regularly cloak their actions. In August 2017 President Morales got on the right track when he declared CICIG commissioner Velásquez unwelcome in Guatemala, under the Vienna Convention on Diplomatic Relations that allows any chief executive to declare any diplomat, for any reason, persona non grata.

In a world that actually honored the concepts of sovereignty and diplomacy, the president's persona non grata order would have gained the respect it deserved. But in the feral conditions that now prevail, the president's order incited protest outside the country; while Guatemala's Constitutional Court immediately, and in violation of the Constitution, vetoed the expulsion of the CICIG commissioner. At present, the CICIG is a hostile sovereign entity that threatens Guatemala from within. Not even the country's chief executive is

PART 1

permitted to restrain the CICIG, or to counter its runaway power. Now more than ever, Guatemalans need an institutional remedy against an "anti-corruption commission" which has despoiled their freedoms, has taken life wantonly, and has redoubled the chaos and lawlessness of their society.

PART 2:
THE PRESIDENT VS THE COMMISSIONER

When Is a Diplomat Not a Diplomat?

The facts

On August 27, 2017, Guatemala's President Jimmy Morales declared Iván Velásquez, commissioner of the UN-created International Commission Against Impunity in Guatemala (CICIG), to be persona non grata and ordered him out of the country.

The president's power to designate as persona non grata a foreign person, especially a diplomat, is the customary right of any nation and its head of state. The 1961 Vienna Convention on Diplomatic Relations, a treaty which almost every nation on earth has joined, says that the power of declaring persona non grata may be invoked at any time, and without explanation.

The Constitution of Guatemala also gives this power to the president of the republic on an exclusive, absolute basis.

Even so, Morales – undoubtedly realizing that this action against the head of the CICIG would raise a firestorm – took special care to state his reasons for it.

According to Morales, Velásquez had meddled in Guatemala's internal affairs, in violation of the Vienna convention that says the first obligation of diplomats is never to interfere in the business of the host country.

The president asserted that the CICIG commissioner had abused his power on numerous occasions; by illegally putting pressure on Guatemala's Congress, and by making public accusations against

CRIMES WITHOUT PUNSHIMENT
Guatemalan citizens in a manner that violated their rights.

The Agreement Between the United Nations and the State of Guatemala, in establishing the CICIG, defined its commissioner and all its personnel as diplomats; thereby entitling them to diplomatic protections and benefits as defined by the Vienna convention.

The principal benefit was one of immunity; the commissioner and the CICIG staff could not be punished or prosecuted for any of their actions in Guatemala.

The CICIG had invoked diplomatic immunity, at least once, to fend off a charge of murder. On October 28, 2016, the CICIG had staged a raid that ended with the killing of a private citizen in his own home, at an early morning hour when police operations against any residence are forbidden by law.

For that transgression, the CICIG pled diplomatic immunity. As of this writing, the case is still under review; but any judicial verdict against the CICIG is unlikely because, in the persona non grata matter, Guatemala's highest court found the CICIG commissioner to be above the president's power and above the nation's law.

The same day as the president's non grata order, two third-party individuals petitioned the court to grant relief to Velásquez, who never even had to plead on his own behalf. The court immediately granted a temporary injunction against the president's order, gliding over the fact that the third-party petitions were legally insufficient; by law, only the aggrieved party can file for relief.

Two days later, Guatemala's human-rights ombudsman, Jordán Rodas, filed another injunction request against the non grata declaration. The court chose that moment to make its injunction permanent.

But Rodas's part in the matter was not disinterested; he had been identified by the Associated Press as having attended the pro-CICIG demonstration that took place after publication of the president's order. Can one, in good faith, protest as a private citizen and then execute to the same effect as a public official? Only in a context of official corruption.

As it happens, Rodas's injunction request was an act beyond the duties of his office; hence, illegal. In a rule-of-law society, he would have been removed from office and perhaps prosecuted. But since the CICIG is now making law in Guatemala, and since Rodas is on the side of the CICIG, he is showered with honors.

The Fantasy: Sometimes a Diplomat, Sometimes Not

In its decision, the high court raised issues that would kindly be called diversionary; for example, that in creating the CICIG, Guatemala had pledged to enter a dispute-resolution process if any conflict were to arise.

President Morales saw no dispute at all in this matter. The non grata decision was his and his alone to make – a matter beyond conflict or dispute. In Anglo-Saxon legal parlance, a president's declaration of persona non grata is black-letter law – a rule not subject to argument or debate.

To make the matter immediate, we may look at a recent use of the persona non grata statute. On March 15, 2018 British Prime Minister Theresa May ordered the expulsion of 23 Russian diplomats, immediately following a nerve-gas attack in a British city that the British and other governments blamed on Russia. The Russian government might argue with the contention but could not protest the expulsion, because every sovereign state has the right to expel diplomats with no questions asked.

Except for Guatemala; or so says the country's highest court.

CRIMES WITHOUT PUNISHMENT

In facing the incontrovertible use of persona non grata by Guatemala's president, the magistrates of the Constitutional Court needed to have things both ways. For circumstances that benefited Velásquez's diplomatic standing, they needed him to be a diplomat; while for circumstances like the non grata order which made Velásquez's diplomatic standing inconvenient, they needed him to be not a diplomat as well.

The magistrates were crafty enough to avoid putting this idea into words. It would have contradicted the CICIG's founding document, which designates the CICIG's members as diplomats; and it would have denied the visible fact that the CICIG, in other situations, has claimed diplomatic immunity.

Anyway, the high court's reticence paid off. By keeping quiet on this matter, the court allowed Velásquez and the CICIG to be both things at once.

The court's real position was most clearly disclosed in its honoring of the injunction request from the human-rights ombudsman, which portrayed Velásquez as an ordinary citizen whose rights were being trampled by Guatemala's president.

On its face, the court's permanent injunction against Morales was out of order. The affected parties were given no chance to present evidence and arguments; indeed, they could not have had that chance within the two days it took for the court to publish its decision.

On October 10, 2017, the Constitutional Court pronounced the matter closed. The non grata order thereby surmounted, Velásquez was able to stay; and stay he did. The court's decision was politically motivated, consciously illegal, and in clear violation of the right to due process. The CICIG commissioner, whose calling-card is the fight against impunity, knows that he may remain in Guatemala only by virtue of an illegal ruling on his own behalf.

PART 3:
FROM HERE TO ETERNITY

THE CICIG PROSECUTES THE PAVÓN PRISON CASES

In 1996 the Government of Guatemala took two decisions exemplifying the view that "tomorrow is a better day." One of these was to stop the country's internal conflict with a faulty truce. The second decision, less well-known, turned out no better. The government gave up control of its toughest prison, Pavón, and allowed its inmates to run the place, while it merely policed the perimeter.

Authorities called it an experiment in self-government. But it created a genuine house of horrors, perhaps best documented in accounts by The Sydney Morning Herald.

Ten years later, in 2006, the government of President Oscar Berger decided to re-take the prison by force. The battle, pitting some 3,000 government troops against 1,500 of Latin America's toughest inmates, ended with the loss of seven prisoner lives and the dispersal of surviving prisoners to other penal facilities.

Given the inherent violence in the situation, one might say that seven lives lost was a low number. Indeed, Guatemala's human-rights ombudsman – which often criticizes the government – called the Pavón takeover a job well done.

Later, however, the ombudsman claimed that a conspiracy had existed to kill specific prisoners, and recommended to Berger's successor that he put the CICIG ("International Commission Against Impunity in Guatemala") on the case. Neither party needed urging: President Álvaro Colom was an ardent admirer of the CICIG's, while the CICIG was a prosecutorial machine waiting to bring charges.

As it happens, the CICIG's prosecutions in the Pavón cases have been inconsistent at best and fishy at worst. The bottom line registers most tellingly: after nine years of prosecutorial activity on both sides of the Atlantic, with millions of dollars wasted and many lives disrupted, the CICIG – despite some interim rulings in its favor – has not been able to sustain a single conviction.

The Hunt Continues: Prosecuting Erwin Sperisen

One of the cases – thanks to the CICIG's endless appetite for appealing its losses – remains unresolved as of this writing. Working with a group of self-described human-rights activists in Switzerland eight years ago, the CICIG managed to cobble together an effective prosecution of Erwin Sperisen, who had been Guatemala's chief of police at the time of Pavon's recapture.

Sperisen, a dual citizen of Switzerland and Guatemala, was convicted of extra-judicial execution and spent five years in solitary confinement in a Swiss prison – treated as though he were a Nazi war criminal, which is how the CICIG and the human-rights activists had managed to paint him.

In June 2017, Switzerland's highest court determined that Sperisen's rights to a defense and to due process had been violated. The high court freed him from jail and ordered a new trial to begin in April 2018. But the conditions of the new trial do not augur well for justice. A fact of overriding significance is that the judge and prosecutor in the new trial will be the same persons who played those roles in the fraudulent trial that sent Sperisen to jail. The prosecutor is actually the son of the man who founded the human-rights group behind Sperisen's troubles. Evidently, Switzerland is the small country that it seems.

In the new trial, a crucial decision of the court will be how it treats two pieces of evidence that the CICIG, for a decade, has kept suppressed. During the trial in Austria of Sperisen's former assistant

Javier Figueroa, the court allowed the defense to show a video of the prison takeover – a video kept under wraps by the CICIG – which shows unmistakably that a gun-battle occurred. That fact fatally exposes the charge of extra-judicial execution, which requires that the victim be under the total control of his killers.

Likewise, attorneys for Sperisen are certain to raise another video made by a Swiss journalist, showing that the CICIG had fraudulently extracted testimony from the mother of a prisoner who died during the Pavón gun-battle. First time around, the Swiss court that convicted Sperisen rejected this evidence, in which the mother disavowed a French-language power of attorney that the court accepted. The video makes clear that she had signed it, at the CICIG's insistence, without understanding the language; a fact that renders her testimony invalid.

One would have to say that the odds are poor for Sperisen in facing the same judge and prosecutor who convicted him in the earlier, tainted trial. Zealots who place politics before justice have poor records for openness and flexibility. That observation goes twice or more for the CICIG.

Alejandro Giammattei

In Guatemala, the prosecutorial axe fell on Alejandro Giammattei, director of the national penitentiary system. The justice ministry, with the CICIG calling the shots, indicted him for "extrajudicial execution" or murder at Pavón and at another prison. A subsidiary charge in the indictment was "illicit association" or conspiracy to do murder.

The prosecutorial conduct of the CICIG was anti-legal in nature. Prosecutors held testimony hearings without notifying the defense, which saw the bulk of the prosecution's evidence only minutes before Giammattei was to appear in court. Meanwhile, the CICIG's website portrayed Giammattei variously as a kidnapper, a paid assassin, an extortionist, a money launder and a drug trafficker – even though none of those crimes had been imputed to him.

The CICIG's chief witness against Giammattei was one of his deputies, retired Lieut. Col. Luis Linares, who coordinated the government's effort to re-take Pavón prison. In that operation, the prison guards were to wait until other forces had re-established order inside. So Giammattei gave the order for guards not to carry arms when entering the prison.

It emerged that Linares had disobeyed this order and told one of his own men to withdraw two weapons and 90 rounds of ammunition from the guards' armory. According to testimony, Linares entered with the invading force and fired his weapon. The CICIG's own report said casings found at the crime scene were 7.62 mm caliber, the same as had been given to Linares's man.

The CICIG hid this exculpatory evidence from the defense. It didn't investigate weapons taken from the armory without authorization; and it didn't investigate the weapons Linares and his man had carried during the raid.

After two days of testimony, the trial judge dismissed the murder charges against Giammattei. Seven months later, he went to trial on the conspiracy charge. When prosecutors affirmed that the conspiracy had begun on "a day in June 2006," the judge noted a lack of specificity as to places, dates or times that the accused had supposedly met to plan their crime. The judge also noted that the law against illicit association had not been in existence at the time the defendants were supposed to be violating it.

The judge ordered the case closed and the defendants freed. That was the cue for the CICIG to begin its cycle of appeals. The appeals court upheld the judge's decision, but then the justice ministry appealed to the Supreme Court, the country's second-highest, which favored the CICIG over the defendants.

The defense petitioned the country's highest judicial body, the Constitutional Court, for an injunction against the Supreme Court ruling. On July 18, 2012 the high court – which was not yet completely under the CICIG's control – favored the defendants, with a rebuke to the Supreme Court. That court was then obliged to uphold the defendants' appeal and grant their dismissal.

Prosecution in Spain

It was finally a prosecution in Spain that crushed any doubts about the CICIG's tactics and motives in the case. In October 2010, four years after the events at Pavón, former Interior Minister Carlos Vielmann was arrested in Spain, where he also held citizenship and where he was living. At the request of Guatemala's justice ministry and the CICIG, a local court charged Vielmann with murder and conspiracy in the Pavón killings. He was released on bail, pending trial.

After a further five-year delay, Vielmann's trial began in Spain in November 2015. Despite the dismissal of those same charges against Giammattei years earlier and a 2013 not guilty verdict in Austria of former assistant police director Javier Figueroa, the CICIG had decided to use its worldwide prosecutorial power against a man who – given his position as Interior Minister – would have been nowhere near the killings.

For the Spanish trial, the CICIG also trotted out its old witness, former Lieut. Col. Luis Linares. He testified that the conspirators – Vielmann and others – had a list of prisoners whom they had marked for execution.

In response to the CICIG and Guatemala's justice ministry, Vielmann filed a civil suit in Spain against sixteen parties in rebuttal to "false and humiliating charges" launched against him in a YouTube video entitled "Impunity: Guatemala Report." Among the defendants were the CICIG commissioner and staff, and Guatemalan justice minister

CRIMES WITHOUT PUNSHIMENT
Claudia Paz y Paz.

The trial court in Spain did not see things as the CICIG would have wanted. The Spanish judge all but called Linares a paid witness, noting that he resided in Canada with a pension from the CICIG. The court rejected his testimony, and that of other prosecution witnesses, as lacking credibility and as having the appearance of being tainted. Instead, the court resurrected a view of the Pavón events that had been current at the time. The deaths, it said, were part of a violent confrontation, and the human-rights ombudsman had been right to praise the operation. The court said it could not find "any proof of a designed plan by the government of Guatemala for physical elimination [of persons]."

With the exception of Sperisen's case in Switzerland, still ongoing, that completes the balance-sheet of the CICIG and its nine years of work on the Pavón killings. Due to its privileged position – its ability to prosecute anyone, anywhere, with no accountability – it consistently failed to learn from its mistakes and kept repeating them. Everywhere it went, it brought the same tainted witnesses and discredited testimony, trying to obtain convictions that it could not win in Guatemala itself.

A colloquial definition of insanity is that of trying the same failed tactic again and again, expecting it to yield a different result this time. The definition, if not the word, fits the CICIG perfectly in these cases.

PART 4:
THE CASE OF THE DISAPPEARING ATTORNEY GENERAL

In the spring of 2010, the government of Guatemalan president Álvaro Colom, two years in power, was preparing to choose an attorney general – a semi-independent office which functions apart from the rest of the executive branch.

A nominating commission – comprised of law school deans, bar association officials, and the president of the Supreme Court – would choose six finalists for the post; the president would then name the winner. Several dozen applicants submitted their papers; among them Conrado Reyes, a 46-year-old attorney with extensive experience inside the government and out.

Evaluations of the candidates, and comments from the commissioners as well as other citizens – the so-called "honorability" phase of the nominating process – became a controversial matter. On May 11 the Constitutional Court, Guatemala's highest judicial body, directed the nominating commission to conduct the honorability phase in public, with a voice vote – thereby exposing this matter for the first time to open view.

No one in this public process voiced a negative report against Conrado Reyes; and significantly, neither did the powerful UN "anti-impunity" commission, known by its Spanish acronym CICIG.
Reyes scored a perfect 100 on the list of official criteria. He jumped to the head of the list and the president chose him for the office, which Reyes assumed on May 25.

Legal disputes persisted, however, around the workings of the honorability phase. On June 10, 17 days into Reyes's term, an accredited third party petitioned the Constitutional Court to declare the honorability phase invalid and order it repeated – on grounds that the nominating commission had not performed it in line with the court's earlier order.

That same day, the court issued an opinion which voided not just the honorability phase but the entire selection process. The effect was to cancel Reyes's tenure. On June 11, the high court notified Reyes that he must quit an office which he had held for less than three weeks.

What was going on?

The New York Times reported on June 12 that Carlos Castresana, the head of the anti-impunity commission, had "resigned in frustration, citing the appointment of Mr. Reyes, who he said had links to drug traffickers and illegal adoption rings."

Why had the CICIG commissioner not stated this concern during the honorability phase, only a short while before?

The CICIG's damaging report was backed up by no solid evidence, as President Colom himself affirmed. According to The Times: "The evidence did not prove any wrongdoing by Mr. Reyes, Mr. Colom said, but involved people surrounding him that would have raised 'tremendous doubts' about his selection."

Guatemala's high court had evidently been in a great hurry to throw Reyes out of office. From start to finish, the court's entire deliberation of the case took a mere eight hours, which analysts later said was far too short a time to honor all the procedures that the law required.

In essence, a sitting attorney general had been expelled from his post on the basis of gossip. The land's highest court had joined the president in perpetrating a judicial fraud. Also pushing the fraud along were the vaunted anti-impunity commission and the US ambassador.

PART 4
Quick Work

Guatemalan attorney José Luis González, a recognized expert in constitutional matters, supplied missing parts of the narrative when, six years after the fact, he recounted his talk with a magistrate – or judge – of the high court.

"I personally heard from one of the magistrates, and in the presence of another two witnesses, about the conversation in which [US Ambassador Stephen] McFarland and Mr. Castresana, the head of [the CICIG], told the magistrates to dismiss Conrado Reyes because, supposedly, he had links to criminal organizations. That magistrate told me the story right to my face. He said he asked them for proof, and told them he could not decide without proof. And they told him: 'Look, this is public knowledge. We have the proof and we are going to send it to you. But you need to take action now, because this is a very serious matter.'"

"Six years later," González added, "that magistrate is still waiting to see the proof – because, of course, no such thing existed."

The reasons for the removal of Conrado Reyes, one of the strangest official transactions in this hemisphere, have never been disclosed. But a telling fact is that Reyes himself, after the event, was never accused of any crime. Nor was a complaint raised against him when he later applied for judgeships on Guatemala's two highest courts.
A plausible view of these events lies elsewhere – with Reyes's successor, and in how she got to the office.

Claudia Paz y Paz was an activist attorney and a Marxist sympathizer, known and liked by President Colom's "in-crowd" for her work in the UN and other transnational groups. She became justice minister six months after Reyes's removal, in a process distinct from the original contest.

If, in June 2010, the high court had invalidated only the honorability phase as petitioned, Reyes might have held onto the post; while Paz y Paz, not a part of the earlier candidate group, couldn't have entered the process. By decreeing a total re-do, the court effectively opened the way for her.

Attorney Moisés Galindo, a defense attorney who crossed swords with Paz y Paz, said of her during her term as minister: "She is the attorney general by law, but she did not get there legitimately. It was a fraudulent maneuver by the UN commission, which pushed Guatemala's institutions to remove the prior attorney general. Then, under the umbrella of the same UN commission, her supporters in civil society propelled her into office."

It's quite possible that the real powers had wanted Paz y Paz for minister all along; while Reyes, a good and honorable man, had been chosen to play the fall guy.

Epilogue

In 2014, as her term at the ministry was ending, Paz y Paz tried for reappointment. President Obama's ambassador, against all diplomatic protocol, urged that she be given a full second term. But not even the power of the US could put Paz y Paz on the list of six names forwarded to President Otto Pérez by the nominating commission.
At the time of her replacement, Paz y Paz was prosecuting various cases against military veterans stemming from Guatemala's internal armed conflict (1960-1996). The cases were based on fabricated evidence, and the ministry pushed them forward with gross violations of due process. Paz y Paz's ministry had been loaded with such perpetrations – a fact that likely caused the president's commission, a body of lawyers, to keep her off the nominations list. President Pérez chose Thelma Aldana as the new justice minister. The CICIG – despite having opposed Aldana for the Supreme Court four years earlier, calling her corrupt – now made no objections to her.

PART 4

Since becoming minister, Aldana has worked hand-in-glove with CICIG commissioner Iván Velásquez. She has continued Paz y Paz's cases against the former officers with help from the CICIG, even though the cases are far outside the CICIG's mandate.

PART 5:
SOVIET SHOW-TRIALS IN THE AMERICAS

THE CASE OF THE CICIG VERSUS MOISÉS GALINDO

The CICIC Sets Up a Defense Attorney

Moisés Galindo is a criminal defense attorney who, in high-profile matters, has defended clients against prosecution by the International Commission Against Impunity in Guatemala (CICIG). Galindo has also represented persons making charges against the CICIG.

On October 4, 2017 the justice ministry's "special division against impunity," attached to the CICIG, brought to court one of Galindo's clients, Alexandra Reyes, for the purpose of gathering a sworn statement. The session was to take place before the same judge who was presiding over a case in which the witness, Reyes, was being defended by Galindo.

The basis of the October hearing was a July 11, 2017 meeting between Reyes and Galindo, which Reyes had initiated at the CICIG's behest. Galindo took the meeting without knowing that the CICIG was behind it.

Likewise, Galindo was kept in the dark about Reyes's later testimony before the trial judge.

The judge, Erica Aifan, obviously knew that Reyes was testifying about matters that were subject to lawyer-client confidentiality. Not only did Judge Aifan let the testimony proceed; she granted an arrest warrant against Galindo as soon as Reyes had concluded her testimony. These facts made Judge Aifan complicit in the irregular procedure.

CRIMES WITHOUT PUNISHMENT
Reyes's Testimony & Galindo's Arrest

In her statement, according to prosecution filings, Reyes testified that Galindo had received a vehicle from her co-defendant as payment for legal fees. Reyes claimed Galindo had told her that the vehicle given in payment was part of an illicit transaction.

Reyes testified she had recorded the talk at the CICIG's request, with a bracelet recorder the CICIG had supplied to her. Reyes also testified that she had already acted as an agent for the CICIG in this way – meeting another person and bringing a recorder to the meeting.

At the end of Reyes's statement, prosecutor Juan Sandoval – accused by Galindo in another criminal process – asked the judge to order Galindo's arrest. The judge complied.

Galindo was arrested the following day and charged with money-laundering for having received the vehicle. On his way into court, Galindo was forced to pass through a gauntlet of reporters – an act expressly prohibited by Article 13 of the Constitution.

Justice Minister Thelma Aldana and CICIG Commissioner Iván Velásquez also met with the press at that time, and spoke about the charges against Galindo as if they were proven facts.

Immediately upon the judge's detention order, the justice ministry and the CICIG began the seizure of all Galindo's material assets.

Alleging illegalities against him, Galindo twice filed habeas corpus motions; both were immediately denied. As of this writing, Judge Aifan has not yet complied with her legal obligation to deliver to the defense a usable copy of the recording that Reyes says she made of her meeting with Galindo. A sound-file of some kind was given to the defense, but it was so garbled that it had no meaning whatever. The prosecution's failure to produce a true sound-record of the meeting leaves doubt as to whether such a thing actually exists.

PART 5
Irregularities in the Case

Hardly anything about this case, except perhaps the courtroom furnishing, has been in conformity with applicable law.
- No judge had authorized any recording that Reyes and the CICIG might have produced.
- During the first four weeks after Galindo's arrest, supposedly incriminating information on his case was distributed to news media without Galindo having been allowed – as the law requires – to examine it.
- In efforts to justify the many delays over Galindo's arraignment, Judge Aifan made various excuses to the effect that her schedule was overcrowded, or that no courtroom was available to hold the hearing.
- While Judge Aifan permitted the press, illegally, to accost Galindo for one hour, she expelled Karen Ness, a US-Guatemalan citizen, from the courtroom area as she recorded the press committing the illegal action.
- On November 6, Judge Aifan received the prosecution – justice ministry and CICIG representatives – for about 45 minutes in her chambers without the presence of the defense. This occurred before the continuation of Galindo's arraignment.

Points of Legal Analysis

Galindo's imprisonment is illegal because the court, the justice ministry and the CICIG have grossly violated his rights to due process.

The arrest warrant against Galindo was granted immediately after the state's witness had testified, and despite the absence of any proof that a crime had been committed.

Galindo was held for fifty-seven days under what the justice ministry called "provisional confinement." This concept does not exist in Guatemala's juridical order.

The violation of the attorney-client privilege, and the lack of a court order for recording the July 11 meeting, make any record about the meeting – be it a recording or witness testimony – inadmissible as evidence. Even so, Judge Aifan cited the supposed recording as grounds for all her rulings in the case, which include the arrest warrant and Galindo's continued detention.

The courts did not treat Galindo's request for relief or his habeas corpus motions in a lawful manner. The judge delayed the former for a month; and as for the latter, a higher court ignored the obvious violations of due process by the lower court.

Despite the Constitution's numerous guarantees of private property and due process, the CICIG and the justice ministry began the process of confiscating all Galindo's assets. They and the court have also violated Galindo's lawful rights, as enumerated in many articles of the Constitution.

Further Conclusions

Through their public statements as well as leaks to the media, the CICIG and ministry of justice, in advance of any bona fide legal process, have already made out Galindo to be guilty as charged.

The 2016 report of the UN's human rights commissioner in Guatemala complained about abuses of preventive detention as a political weapon against citizens. The UN's own CICIG, as well as the justice ministry, have been the protagonists in many such cases. Moisés Galindo's is one of those.

It is hard to avoid the conclusion that Guatemala's justice ministry, with the CICIG as chief instigator, deprived Moisés Galindo of his freedom and his constitutional rights as retribution for his earlier work in opposing their own legal and ethical violations and as an attempt to intimidate their opposition, including defense lawyers.

PART 6:
SEVEN YEARS IN PRISON
FOR NOTHING AT ALL

THE CASE OF THE VALDÉS PAIZ BROTHERS
Guatemala, May 2009–November 2017

2009: Murder or Suicide?

On May 10, 2009, attorney Rodrigo Rosenberg was shot to death near his home in Guatemala City. One day later, a video appeared on social media in which Rosenberg – seeming to speak from the beyond – said his death had been caused by President Álvaro Colom, First Lady Sandra Torres and their associates.

The month before Rosenberg died, two of his clients – Khalil Musa and Musa's daughter Marjorie – had been gunned down in the capital. The elder Musa, a businessman, was also a director of Banrural or Guatemala's development bank, a position to which President Colom had appointed him.

In the video, Rosenberg claimed that President Colom, First Lady Sandra Torres and their associates had been using Banrural to embezzle and launder money. Musa was killed, or so Rosenberg said, because he had objected to the corruption.

From the grave, and thanks to the magic of social media, Rosenberg was demanding Colom's resignation. His call, broadcast on national TV, inspired large-scale protests that put Colom's presidency in danger.

The president vehemently denied the claims and called on the CICIG to investigate.

CRIMES WITHOUT PUNSHIMENT

The CICIG and President Colom

The International Commission Against Impunity in Guatemala (CICIG) is a branch of the UN that works through Guatemala's justice ministry. According to its mandate, the CICIG "carries out independent investigations into the activities of illegal security groups and clandestine security structures," defined as groups that "affect the Guatemalan people's enjoyment and exercise of their fundamental human rights."

By September 2009, police had arrested nine men who were charged with Rosenberg's killing. But the CICIG was not to be ignored. In November 2009 it issued a report saying its own investigation had revealed the possible participation of Francisco and Estuardo Valdés Paiz, bothers who were businessmen in the pharmaceutical field.

Those brothers were cousins of Rosenberg's ex-wife. The CICIG stated an unusual, not to say eccentric, theory of the case. It alleged that the Valdés brothers had actually hired the killers at Rosenberg's behest. In a nutshell, the CICIG was claiming that Rosenberg had committed suicide by means of contract killers, with the aim of bringing down Colom's government.

The CICIG was evidently trying to get Colom off the hook and save his presidency. If that was the aim, it worked.

The Case Unfolds

In December 2009, taking direction from the CICIG which it termed a "co-plaintiff," the justice ministry requested the arrest of the Valdés Paiz brothers. Its case was based entirely on testimony by witnesses in prison.

In response, the Valdés brothers presented a motion to let them see the evidence. The responsible court denied the motion.

PART 6

On June 28, 2010, the Valdés brothers surrendered at the CICIG's office. The expropriation of their assets – a CICIG trademark tactic against its targets – quickly began; and the brothers were confined to the prison at the Mariscal Zavala military base, where they were to await trial.

Almost from the start, the case went badly for the CICIG. The prosecution moved to raise the charge from murder to assassination, but Judge Veronica Galicia denied the motion. After some controversy, Galicia recused herself from the case and turned it over to Judge Carlos Aguilar.

Almost immediately the CICIG moved for the recusal of Judge Aguilar, claiming that he bore the CICIG a grudge and was a personal enemy of the CICIG's commissioner. Aguilar, for his part, stated in early 2012 that the CICIG did not have a mandate to involve itself in the case, which he termed an ordinary criminal matter.

The CICIG's motion to recuse Aguilar was rejected. The CICIG repeated its motion twice more and was refused each time. These cycles of motion-and-rejection added many months to the judicial process.

After losing the third recusal, Guatemala's Supreme Court granted the CICIG an injunction, which froze the case. Just days later, on November 30, 2012, the CICIG published a statement in which it accused Aguilar and five other judges of favoring criminal groups opposed to the CICIG's presence in the country.

Now that the CICIG had picked a public fight with Aguilar, he could no longer appear to be objective and was obligated to excuse himself; on January 14, 2013, he took himself off the case. The commissioners then showed themselves to be sore winners – by gloating, on their website, that the Supreme Court had found fault with Aguilar's objectivity. All along the CICIG knew it could apply its smears without consequence, thanks to the prior grant of diplomatic immunity which automatically protected everything, no matter how lowly or despicable, that the commission might do.

For all its swagger, however, the CICIG could not keep the tables from turning against its flawed case. On July 13, 2013, state's witness Manuel Cardona retracted his testimony against the Valdés brothers, saying he had been coerced by the CICIG and by justice ministry prosecutors to accuse the brothers falsely.

The point was made again in early 2014 when state's witness Luis Paz also retracted his testimony, which he said had been coerced by the CICIG.

For the next three years, the CICIG's lawyers filed a stream of frivolous motions whose only effect was to keep the Valdés brothers unjustly confined. Finally, on May 11, 2017 Judge Mynor Moto said he would free the brothers within three months if prosecutors failed to offer proof of a crime.

With no proof forthcoming, Judge Moto on August 28 dismissed the case against the Valdés brothers for lack of evidence. The brothers were free, having spent more than seven years in jail for nothing at all. The justice ministry appealed, but in November 2017 the appeals court confirmed Moto's ruling.

Some days after its appeal had failed, the CICIG announced it was bringing charges against Judge Moto for his actions in another case, in which he had also ruled against the CICIG.

Observations

The legal process was flawed from the beginning, as soon as the defendants were denied access to evidence that the prosecution claimed to have. Especially offensive was the CICIG's use of an extreme tactic: expropriations of the defendants' assets.

PART 6

The violations of due process most notably included coercing imprisoned witnesses to give false testimony.

The CICIG filed a succession of empty motions to "eat up the clock" and keep the defendants languishing in prison.

The commission's releasing a list of judges whom it called corrupt was an obvious act of intimidation against any judge who might be inclined to rule against it.

Thanks to diplomatic immunity, the CICIG commissioners could take any course they chose – no matter how abusive or nonsensical – knowing they would never be held accountable for their actions. The justice ministry, however, can be held accountable. It is still under obligation to charge those of its own staff who broke the law while prosecuting the case.

Conclusion

Had the false-witness statements been an error, prosecutors would have withdrawn the charges. Instead, they delayed; they recused judges and bullied them; they kept the defendants in jail for years after the witnesses had recanted.

The CICIG, enjoying perfect impunity, used this case to remove presumption of innocence from Guatemala's judicial system. With no correspondence to truth, the CICIG set itself up as the guiding authority on who is corrupt and who should go to jail – to the point that almost nobody in authority dares object.

The only way to avoid this judicial terrorism and prevent such abuses in the future is to bind the CICIG to a regime of constant oversight. Given that CICIG personnel are UN-backed diplomats, responsibility for this oversight belongs to the UN – which to date has failed in its duty.

CRIMES WITHOUT PUNSHIMENT

Given the violations of law and justice that occurred in this case alone – a monstrosity over which every one of the CICIG commissioners presided – the president of Guatemala has ample motive, as well as the backing of law, to remove the CICIG at once and throw its personnel out of the country.

PART 7:
THE CICIG IN BRIEF

PROGRESSIVES AGAINST THE FOOLS' BRIGADE

The government of Guatemala and the United Nations agreed in 2006 to create the International Commission Against Impunity in Guatemala (CICIG), a "non-UN organ" that would strengthen the capacity of Guatemala to "fulfill its obligations under the human rights conventions to which it is a party."

The CICIG's stated objectives were to support, strengthen and assist Guatemala's institutions "responsible for investigating and prosecuting crimes allegedly committed in connection with the activities of illegal security forces and clandestine security organizations." Illegal security groups were defined as those that "commit illegal acts in order to affect the full enjoyment and exercise of civil and political rights . . ."

Under the founding agreement, the CICIG would have full license to prosecute crimes alongside the justice ministry. At the same time, the CICIG commissioner and his subordinates would "enjoy the privileges and immunities [of] diplomatic agents in conformity with the 1961 Vienna Conventions on Diplomatic Relations."

The effect of these measures was to give the CICIG unlimited prosecutorial power, combined with full impunity.

Activist groups in Guatemala, so-called progressives, had been trying to create such a commission since the mid-1990's, when peace negotiations brought a halt to the country's 36-year-long internal armed conflict. In 2004 Guatemala's highest judicial body, the Constitutional Court, was asked for an opinion on the idea and responded in the negative.

The court stated that the proposed body would not be a genuine human-rights instrument; further, that it would serve an illegal function if it prosecuted crimes – a task that properly belonged to the justice ministry alone.

Even so, a nearly identical proposal was approved in 2006 by that same court and its new crop of magistrates. On December 12, 2006, Guatemala and the United Nations signed the agreement creating the CICIG.

Pursuant to article 171.1 of the Constitution, President Oscar Berger submitted the agreement to Congress. The key committee voted against it, arguing that it violated the Constitution in several key respects.

But the sovereign wishes of a constitutional republic flew in the face of world opinion. Larger forces from outside were demanding that international law take precedence over sovereignty; they put heavy pressure on Guatemala's leaders to approve the CICIG.

On August 1, 2007 Congress gave in and without debate ratified the agreement, calling it an urgent priority for the nation. The commission's term was for two years, and subject to renewal.

In 2009 Guatemalan President Colom asked Congress to renew the CICIG, and Congress agreed. Since that time Congress has not voted on the CICIG's renewal – yet the CICIG has stayed.

This lapse has been a blatant violation of the Constitution, which requires Congress to "approve, before its ratification, treaties, agreements or any international arrangement" when it affects laws in effect or financially obligates the State.

Congress acted correctly in 2009 when it approved the CICIG's extension. But in 2011, to avoid a possible rejection, the relevant committee didn't take up the issue. When it failed to vote on another extension, Congress acted incorrectly by shirking its responsibility to approve or disapprove international agreements entered into by the president.

The CICIG's existence has been illegal under Guatemalan law since 2011. Yet today – by dint of brute fact instead of law – the CICIG is more entrenched than ever. It has become so by concentrating on the bare-knuckled accumulation of power, while relying on its diplomatic immunity.

The CICIG is no more a diplomatic mission than any other group of international adventurers. The CICIG reports to nobody – not even to its sponsor, the UN.

Guatemala's justice ministry has been the CICIG's base of operation. But the ministry and its staff are subject to national law, while the CICIG is subject to no law or oversight at all. That fact, which everyone in Guatemala's government knows, has given the CICIG the majority of power in the ministry, and at times the major part of power in the country.

The CICIG uses the justice ministry as its mask. Behind the spectacular misuses of power in Guatemalan justice – the frequent use of false witnesses, illegal surveillances, and more – the CICIG is omnipresent. In at least one case, the CICIG compelled a defendant to carry a voice-recorder to a meeting with her own attorney. As a result, the attorney is now sitting in jail.

The CICIG is able to imprison and expropriate any Guatemalan it wishes. It has stood behind at least one murder, in which it avoided prosecution on grounds of diplomatic immunity.

In 2010 its machinations allowed President Colom to unseat a justice minister whom the president had wished to make a fall-guy. By 2015, the CICIG had upped its game to removing and imprisoning the president and vice president. That same year, it cooperated with

President Obama's ambassador in an effort to "postpone" a scheduled presidential election. Ever since then, it has been working to unseat the winner.

By now the CICIG embodies the very impunity it was set up to eliminate. And it functions very much like the "illegal security groups" that it had once pledged to eradicate.

You cannot be in Guatemalan politics without knowing the CICIG's power. Today, the first requirement for holding an office – not only in the justice ministry or on the various courts, but anywhere in the executive branch – is that you have "excellent working relations" with the CICIG.

From its bunker in the justice ministry, the CICIG has placed many friends and displaced many adversaries in judgeships at every level. For now the CICIG commands a neat majority, 3-to-2, of the Constitutional Court. That control is nothing less than the ability to say what is law and what is not, as leaders from the president on down are well aware.

The CICIG knows it cannot survive without robust international support. Accordingly, it plays with great skill and care to the global progressive movement, as well as to those portions of Guatemala's populace that naively believe its propaganda. Catch-phrases like "anti-corruption," "human rights," "indigenous rights," and of course "anti-impunity" drop from the CICIG's official statements like overripe fruit.

The uniform CICIG response to its opponents is that they are pro-impunity and pro-corruption. So far this tactic has worked amazingly well. It has worked with the US Department of State – even under President Trump, whose diplomats ought to know better.

The reality of the CICIG is this: if your organization is an official body wielding state power without limitations, without oversight,

PART 7

and without the possibility of punishment, your operation is going to grow undisciplined and sloppy at best; immoral and inhumane at worst.

According to legal analysts, the following methods of operation are present in many of the criminal processes filed and managed by the CICIG and its staff:

- They prosecute cases that provoke public scandal, while not filing cases against persons and groups politically aligned with them.
- They seek the most vulnerable people to serve as witnesses and bribe them. If subjects reject the bribe, the CICIG threatens and coerces them to testify falsely against their, the CICIG's, targets.
- They obtain arrest warrants against their targets based solely on witness testimony, without supporting evidence.
- They create a media circus when they carry out arrests, involving an exaggerated number of police, vehicles, and weapons.
- They force arrestees to walk long distances on their way to court, illegally exposing them to the press and denigrating them.
- They present arrestees in handcuffs as if they were dangerous criminals, regardless of their age or physical disabilities.
- They convene press conferences before arraigning arrestees in which they present the charges as proven facts against which there can be no contrary evidence.
- Somehow, those charged by the CICIG are assigned mostly to judges who accept the CICIG's petitions without objection. Those judges delay arraigning arrestees in violation of their rights, sometimes for several months.
- The CICIG and its staff deny the accused access to the evidence against them, and allow defense lawyers only minutes to review evidence before having to respond. They withhold evidence in some cases until after taking the accused's statement, in violation of the law.

- When CICIG-friendly judges aren't assigned to cases because they are too busy, other judges often rule against the CICIG which, whenever that happens, immediately recuses the judge. The CICIG then puts the recused on a list of corrupt judges. If an appeals court should confirm an anti-CICIG ruling, the CICIG seeks to remove and jail the ruling judge for crimes he or she didn't commit.
- Defense lawyers in CICIG cases routinely denounce illegal detention, violations of the right to a defense, violations of due process, denial of the presumption of innocence, failure to adhere to time requirements for actions and, especially, illegal prolongation of their clients' detention.
- Victims of CICIG persecution have publicly denounced the extraordinary cruelty of punishments designed to break their will and force them, against the truth, to admit guilt.

Up to now, the CICIG's opponents have had an extremely hard time fighting against it; while fighting against the CICIG plus the United States, as at least one member of Guatemala's Congress has learned, is a fool's errand.

Congressman Fernando Linares wrote a letter to Secretary of State John Kerry, detailing the CICIG's violations of diplomacy and law. He never received a reply. Due to his opposition in Congress to the CICIG and to US policy, he became a marked man. In April 2017, the US consulate peremptorily cancelled his right to travel to the US – an insult to someone of his standing. For more, see the account of his case in Part 9 of this series.

Even so, the CICIG's tactics have been so blatant and unappealing that a fools' brigade has started to form. It now includes the president of the republic.

The CICIG and its allies are appropriately concerned. As of this writing, the Constitutional Court has been asked to declare that the agreement with the UN establishing the CICIG should become

PART 7

part of the country's permanent law – not subject to review by the people's Congress.

There is no reason in that view; only desperation.

PART 8:
THE CICIG AND GUATEMALA'S CONSTITUTION

The CICIG

The most significant presence in Guatemala's recent governance has been the International Commission Against Impunity, best known by its Spanish-language acronym CICIG.

According to the United Nations, which invented the commission and its mandate, the CICIG "aims to investigate illegal security groups and clandestine security organizations in Guatemala – criminal groups believed to have infiltrated state institutions, fostering impunity and undermining democratic gains . . . ."

The CICIG enjoys diplomatic immunity and other privileges of diplomatic status. By the same token, and on paper anyway, it is subject to diplomatic limitations. The first of these is that no diplomat may interfere in the ordinary workings of the host country.

In 2015, CICIG commissioner Iván Velásquez started a series of "dialogue tables" in which he invited a series of citizen groups to construct a campaign for changing Guatemala's constitution.

Such were the CICIG's prestige and power that rather few people asked the obvious question. As a diplomatic entity, what business did the CICIG have in planning changes to Guatemala's constitution, or to its social order?

The Battle in Congress

In 2016 President Jimmy Morales announced that he himself would send the CICIG proposals to Congress. Without explaining his reasons, Morales did not follow up on this pledge. But a number of participants commented that the CICIG's text was different from what had been approved in the discussions.

The CICIG's response was to direct the justice ministry to file corruption charges against Morales's son and brother.

In Congress, 52 members sponsored the CICIG's proposals. After easily approving a few articles, Congress confronted the CICIG's major initiative: to replace Guatemala's unitary justice system with a myriad of zones which would observe "indigenous rights" and "ancestral authorities."

The effect, in a poor nation with manifold ethnic differences, would have been to impose a legal regime of "different strokes for different folks."

CICIG commissioner Velásquez, Attorney General Thelma Aldana and Human Rights Ombudsman Jorge De León attended the session of Congress at which members debated the controversial article. Despite the heavy-handed presence of those authorities, the measure failed to gain the necessary votes.

Velásquez took to meeting with party leaders in hotels – the very definition of "lobbying" – while national and international media reported that US Ambassador Todd Robinson was working in his own way to garner support for the proposals.

The CICIG next proposed to change the Constitution's procedure for appointing judges. A National Judiciary Board was proposed in which, among other things, lower-court judges and lay persons would nominate judges for the highest courts.

The members of the proposed board would have power over all judiciary nominations. The effect would be to upset the balance that the Constitution had carefully crafted in its separation of powers.

In its place would be a judicial monolith, with all power given to the present occupants of judicial posts—those occupants nearly all partisans of the CICIG.

In a word, the CICIG would be running the judicial branch of government, and the judicial branch would have dominion over the other branches.

This proposal generated so much opposition that its partisans never even tried to bring it to a vote.

The Political Battle

Congressman Fernando Linares requested an injunction against Velásquez attending sessions of Congress, on grounds that no foreigner – Velasquez being a Colombian national – could take part in Guatemala's congressional matters.

Linares also sought an injunction against Aldana's uninvited presence in Congress, which he termed an effort to intimidate the deputies. Shortly thereafter, Aldana presented a criminal complaint against Linares, thereby proving his point about intimidation.

The attorney general's brief accused Linares of discrimination on grounds that, as a member of Congress, he had spoken against a bill which would allocate funds to groups helping disabled persons. The attorney general further demanded that Congress revoke Linares's immunity from prosecution, so he could be criminally charged.

This was an open attack on Linares's rights as a member of Congress; the ministry demanded removal of the Constitution's allowance that congresspersons freely express their opinions in legislative debates. The United States piled on this effort in an obvious and insidious way. In April 2017 the US consulate, abruptly and without explanation, canceled Congressman Linares's right to travel to the United States. By this time, Donald Trump had become president while

Ambassador Robinson, an Obama appointee, falsely claimed to be representing the president's policies. Congressman Linares, a known Trump partisan, better represented American values than did the US ambassador.

Conclusion

The CICIG's effort to change Guatemala by changing its Constitution turned out a failure. But it perpetrated numerous illegalities.

Following President Morales's decision not to present the CICIG's proposal, fifty-two members of Congress sponsored it. Their sponsorship was illegal because it led them to act as a front for the authors of a foreign intervention – Velásquez and the CICIG.

The attorney general and the human rights ombudsman broke the law in their interventions with Congress, because their offices did not give them the power to propose changes to the Constitution.

The attorney general's charges against the president's brother and son, as well as against Congressman Linares, were illegal for being blatant attempts to bully lawmakers into voting for the CICIG's program.

As for Commissioner Velásquez, his activity did more than simply go beyond the CICIG's mandate. With Attorney General Aldana as his sidekick and US Ambassador Robinson as his sponsor, he misused his position to lead what could easily be described as an attempt to subvert democracy.

PART 9:
THE LAWLESSNESS OF GUATEMALA'S JUSTICE
THE CASE OF CONGRESSMAN FERNANDO LINARES

The Facts

In late 2016 Ivan Velásquez, the chief of the International Commission Against Impunity in Guatemala (CICIG), initiated a project to change Guatemala's constitution . His close collaborator in this effort was Guatemala's justice minister, Thelma Aldana.

On November 24, 2016, Velásquez and Aldana announced at a press conference that they would attend the November 28 session of Congress, at which their proposed changes would come to a vote. On November 26 a member of Congress, Fernando Linares, petitioned Guatemala's highest judicial body, the Constitutional Court, for an injunction barring Velásquez and Aldana from attending the session of Congress. Linares's brief argued that Velásquez, as a foreigner, could not interfere in the country's political affairs; and that his presence at the session, along with Aldana's, would be an attack on Congress's independence.

The high court rejected Linares's petition on grounds that it was technically flawed. Thereby the court violated the law of injunctions, which stipulates in Article 22 that petitions will be admitted and that petitioners will be given time to correct any faults.

In the meantime, Velásquez and Aldana – accompanied by the country's human-rights ombudsman, Jorge de León – did attend the session of Congress at which the CICIG's proposals for constitutional changes were to be put to a vote.

At that session, Congress did not approve the proposals and, against parliamentary procedure, tabled them for future consideration –

thereby putting the matter into stasis. While not frontally barring the efforts of Velásquez and Aldana, Congress was not cooperating in their effort to change the Constitution.

Accordingly, the contest went back to the judicial branch. The Constitutional Court referred Linares's petition to the country's second-highest or Supreme Court, which on December 15 served the CICIG with a demand to answer the petition within two days. The CICIG promptly told the court it rejected the demand, claiming that the CICIG was protected by diplomatic immunity and, hence, could only be enjoined through the Foreign Ministry.

For the court, the CICIG's counter was not a proper response. Therefore it was obliged to grant Linares's request for a temporary injunction. Notably, however, the court gave no publicity to its action, informing neither Linares nor the CICIG that the injunction was in force.

Three months later, presumably after learning of the court's action, the CICIG presented the court with an actual argument against the injunction. The court accepted this brief, despite its having been presented well after the two-day response period had expired.

On the same day the court accepted the CICIG's brief, it notified the plaintiff, Linares, that the temporary injunction had been revoked. Linares appealed. As of this writing, the legal dispute is still in process.

Observations

- The Constitutional Court failed to act immediately, as the law requires, on an injunction to bar outside pressure against Congress.
- The Supreme Court accepted a filing from the CICIG three months after the window for responses had closed.
- More than one year has passed since Linares filed his injunction

request, and it has still not been resolved. This is in stark contrast to the speed with which the Constitutional Court took action against the declaration of persona non grata that President Morales levied against the CICIG commissioner. On that occasion, the court took one day to grant a temporary injunction against the president's order; and only two days to make its injunction effectively permanent.

- The CICIG commissioner's diplomatic status, which that official has utilized to protect himself in court cases, also forbids his meddling in internal affairs. Pressuring members of Congress is an act of meddling.
- Given that Velásquez and Aldana exercise a near-total control over criminal prosecution in Guatemala, members of Congress understandably interpret pressure by those officials as threats against themselves.
- Fernando Linares was a vocal opponent of the changes to the Constitution advocated by Velásquez and Aldana, who in turn had the backing of US ambassador Todd Robinson. The US consulate canceled Linares's US visa and, despite his request, offered no explanation for this unusual action involving a member of Congress.

Linares asserts that the US cancellation of his visa is a punishment for his having opposed the CICIG in this matter. Continuing US silence on this issue has sent an intimidating message to other members of Congress.

Legal Analysis

Article 137 of the Constitution establishes that the right to political petition belongs only to Guatemalans, effectively excluding all foreigners.

Article 10.1 of the agreement between the UN and Guatemala creating the CICIG grants its commissioner diplomatic status – a status, in turn, that makes the commissioner subject to the Vienna

Convention, whose Article 41 expressly prohibits meddling in a host country's internal affairs.

The commissioner's actions in promoting changes to the Constitution went far beyond simple meddling. They were criminal and subversive acts.

According to the Constitution, the justice minister can only perform functions that are specifically mandated by the Constitution. That document does not permit the justice minister to propose constitutional changes. For those reasons, the justice minister exceeded her authority by attending sessions of Congress and thereby pressuring members to vote for the proposed changes.

The gravity of this last point is underlined by the minister having announced possible criminal charges against some members of Congress.

Members of the UNE party were the formal presenters of the proposals to change the Constitution; but it was well established and publicly known that the justice ministry had conceived of the changes and presented them to the UNE – meaning that party acted as a "front organization," which violates the Constitution and its Article 277.

If the rule of law prevailed in Guatemala, Velásquez and Aldana could be charged with abuse of authority, dereliction of duty, usurpation of functions, and constitutional violations. They could also face charges of extortion for having threatened members of Congress to vote for their proposals.

PART 10:
IMPERIALISM IN LATIN AMERICA

OLD WINE IN NEW BOTTLES

Before taking leave of the world stage, Obama administration officials announced the end of US imperialism in Latin America.

American imperialism is "part of the past. It most definitely is part of the past." So said the assistant Secretary of State for Latin America, Roberta Jacobson, who today serves as Donald Trump's ambassador to Mexico.

US policy toward Latin America is no longer couched in terms like hegemony or hemispheric security, which are easily seen as synonyms for US domination. Today's policy arrives in phrases like human rights, women's rights, indigenous rights, respect for the environment, anti-corruption and anti-impunity.

Those concepts are actually being used to attack the sovereignty of independent nations – to reduce their chances of reaching their destinies. No clearer case exists than the persecution of the Oxec hydroelectric companies in Guatemala.

Much of Guatemala today – thanks to help from the United Nations and others from abroad – is dominated by heavily-armed militias which the UN has designated as "human-rights groups" and "indigenous leaders." In many areas of the country, those groups have expelled legitimately-elected officials from power and have supplanted the police and army, which do not dare to challenge them. The militias have their own self-designated justice systems, including clandestine prisons, which they use to intimidate ordinary people. Most consistently, the militia leaders have forbidden development projects in their zones by companies like Oxec; projects that would create wealth, jobs and prosperity for rural peoples.

Those projects would also remove the militias' ability to control the populations they dominate. As it happens, the partisans of international law – who are enamored of slogans like human rights, indigenous rights, and others – have given decisive support to the militias.

In late 2015 Bernardo Caal, an activist who had worked with several of the militias, brought suit against two Oxec projects in the Q'Eqchi indigenous region of north-central Guatemala. Caal asserted that the company had failed to consult the indigenous communities about the projects, as they are required to do by law.

The plaintiff asked the Supreme Court, Guatemala's second-highest judicial body, to cancel the Oxec licenses, claiming the company had not consulted the communities in the manner outlined by Convention 169 of the International Labour Organization (ILO), a UN agency.

Advocates for the company and the ministry vigorously disputed this claim, saying that responsible officials had done exhaustive work in consulting the communities. People from indigenous communities testified that they had indeed been consulted. They said they wanted the projects to proceed.

Those witnesses also said that Caal did not speak for them. Their testimony pulled the rug out from under Caal's claim to represent anyone but himself – and, of course, whatever "indigenous leaders" for whom he might have been fronting.

The court, however, ruled in Caal's favor; whereupon the companies, and Guatemala's Ministry of Energy and Mines, appealed the case to the country's highest judicial body, the Constitutional Court.

PART 10

While the company and the ministry argued facts and law, the plaintiff argued politics. Caal, and the people for whom he was fronting, wanted the court to enshrine their interpretation of ILO Convention 169 as part of Guatemala's national law. And the court delivered a verdict that must have exceeded the plaintiff's wildest dreams.

The Constitutional Court decreed that its interpretation of ILO Convention 169 would henceforth serve as a basis for guidelines in all consultations that include indigenous communities. The court also said that the government would have to meet those standards – not just in the case at hand, but in all future cases.

Further – and here the magistrates really showed their hand – the court issued an order to Congress: within one year, Congress must pass a law setting the conditions under which indigenous communities must receive consultations, in line with the court's decision.

Above all, the Oxec decision showed the members of the country's highest court trying to capture power for the judicial branch – a power that would then be used to make the nation subservient to their interpretation of international law. The high court's decision flatly contradicted Guatemala's ratification of ILO Convention 169, which ruled out any measure inconsistent with the Constitution.

Old-fashioned imperialism used to come from outside. This newfangled imperialism has been getting delivered by the nation's own Constitutional Court – together with the International Commission Against Impunity in Guatemala (CICIG), a UN-appointed agency which is now the dominant power in Guatemala's justice ministry.

Some years ago, the CICIG received a request that it investigate the activities of a "human-rights" militia in the San Marcos region of western Guatemala. That militia, which calls itself the FRENA or "Front for Resistance in Defense of Natural Resources," had supplanted the elected officials of the region and instituted its own tyrannical rule over the citizens of the region.

With the complicity of the central government, FRENA cowed the army and police into inaction. The militia's defining accomplishment was that it had blocked a hydroelectric project and had kept it blocked for several years; an action that spread poverty and encouraged many people to run toward the United States in search of economic opportunity.

In the summer of 2014, citizen groups told visiting reporters from the US that they wished for the hydroelectric project to proceed, and also for law enforcement to be in the hands of police rather than the militia. In a separate conversation with those same reporters, the militia leader – who called himself the "indigenous mayor" of the provincial capital – cited ILO Convention 169 as though it were part of his breviary, which indeed it was.

In 2015, a genuine human-rights activist complained to the CICIG and asked that it investigate the activities of the FRENA militia. The CICIG's mandate is to investigate and dismantle extra-legal armed groups that interfere with basic freedoms and are beyond the reach of the law. That mandate could have been written with reference to an armed body like the FRENA.

But the CICIG commissioner declined this request in a letter which he addressed not to the activist but to justice minister. The commissioner claimed that such an investigation would contravene the CICIG's "need to optimize its available resources during the term of its mandate."

It was a classic bureaucratic dodge that also served the purpose of telling the Justice Ministry to lay off the matter as well. The commissioner later stated that the Justice Ministry "by legal mandate ... must investigate all crimes committed in the country."

PART 10

As matters now stand, the CICIG and the Constitutional Court are aligned for the purpose of inflicting their interpretation of international law on Guatemala. Their choices put the interests of the US – which gives crucial material support to the CICIG – entirely in the dark. By neglecting to take a hard look at its own policy, the US tolerates damage to its own vital interests, while exalting the interests of its enemies.

PART 11:
"OPEN, SESAME!"

THE TRIUMPH OF POLITICS OVER JUSTICE

The late and not-so-lamented Fidel Castro succinctly described the governing principle of Cuba under his rule. "Inside the revolution, everything; outside the revolution, nothing."

In November 2015, shortly after the surprise election that brought Jimmy Morales to power, the new Minister of the Interior appointed retired army Captain Óscar Platero to be assistant director of Civilian Intelligence, or Digici.

Platero, a man strongly qualified for the post, later told journalists that he had worked with the CICIG "at its inception in 2007 . . . because I thought it was going to pursue organized crime." However, he added, the CICIG had been strangely uninterested in the information he supplied.

Given his bad blood with the CICIG, Platero's appointment was controversial. President Alejandro Maldonado told an interviewer he saw no reason for Platero not to serve. But a day after saying so, the president announced through a spokesman that he had ordered the Interior Minister to cancel Platero's appointment.

As the spokesman explained, the Interior Ministry's Digici "is closely related to the Justice Ministry and to the CICIG. This harmony is important, so it's important that those personnel have excellent working relations."

This is now the governing principle at the Justice Ministry, which is the CICIG's official home. In recent years the CICIG has been extending its power through its control of appointments in the judicial branch. The power to select judges enables the CICIG to determine what is law and what is not.

In late 2016 the magistrates of the Supreme Court, Guatemala's second-highest judicial body, chose one of their number, Magistrate Silvia Patricia Valdés, to serve a one-year term as the court's president. But then a pro-CICIG petitioner asked the country's highest judicial body, the Constitutional Court, to void the Valdés appointment on grounds that an alternate magistrate had taken part in the voting.

This was not a case of impartial justice but of politics in command. The CICIG-controlled Constitutional Court voted to oust Valdés from the Supreme Court's presidency, which then went to a magistrate with a record of supporting the choices of the CICIG-controlled Justice Ministry.

In the Constitutional Court's decision against Valdés, not one but two alternates had voted – an irony notoriously ignored by the pro-CICIG party, but well observed by others. At present, the boss of the Constitutional Court is Magistrate Gloria Porras. In June 2010, as a Justice Ministry official, Porras was one of the key players in the abrupt dismissal of Attorney General Conrado Reyes – a judicial fraud perpetrated by CICIG commissioner Carlos Castresana and US Ambassador Stephen McFarland.

The following year, 2011, Porras won appointment to the Constitutional Court. In 2015, the CICIG and the US embassy waged an inappropriate campaign for her reappointment. On orders of Ambassador Todd Robinson, the US embassy bullied Guatemala's Congress to approve a second term for Porras.

On October 3, 2017 the Foundation Against Terrorism presented a criminal complaint against Porras and two government auditors, alleging embezzlement, malfeasance, and other crimes as a result of Porras's having illegally authorized bonuses for court employees. The evidence, a public document signed by Porras, was in black and white.

PART 11

Five days later, instead of passing the case to Congress for the appointment of an investigating commission as the law requires, the Supreme Court rejected the complaint.

In contrast, the Supreme Court had earlier accepted a Justice Ministry case against Congressman Fernando Linares and had immediately appointed an investigating judge.

The matter concerned four disabled people who had lobbied for legislation in Congress. In February 2017 the complainants alleged that Linares had spoken to them in a "disrespectful and arrogant manner, using discriminatory language."

The Constitution states that members of Congress are not liable for "their opinions or initiatives . . . in the performance of their duties." In addition to its general guarantee of free speech, the Constitution specifically protects the rights of congresspersons to speak freely in discharging their duties.

Even so, the Supreme Court ruled that the disabled persons' complaint was legitimate. Notably, Magistrate Silvia Patricia Valdés dissented from the court's ruling.

Despite the patent absurdity of the complaint, its clear violation of the Constitution, and despite a recommendation by the court's own investigating judge against such an action, the Supreme Court voted to strip Linares of his official immunity and render him subject to criminal prosecution.

In accord with Constitutional Court policy, the Supreme Court is now peremptorily deciding the merits of cases before they come to trial. The explicit basis of these decisions is the "immunity" status of the person or persons charged. The underlying criterion is the person's standing with the CICIG.

For Gloria Porras, the Supreme Court upheld her official immunity and threw out the complaint. In the case of Fernando Linares, who is a known adversary of the CICIG and its agenda, the court went 50 country kilometers out of its way to ride roughshod over the Constitution and remove his official immunity. With many judges fearful of the CICIG, Linares is at risk of going to jail.

A curiosity of these judicial pronouncements is the constant use of the Latin phrase "in limine" to ramify the decisions and make them appear legitimate. The phrase simply means, "Now that we are getting under way…" By itself, it confers no authority at all. The law specifies that no court may determine the merits of a case before it is tried. For these uses, the phrase "in limine" has no more legal validity than the magic statement "Open, sesame!" in the story of Ali Baba and the 40 Thieves.

But in a more crucial sense the Open Sesame is rewarding those who have arranged for the triumph of politics over justice.
The CICIG, the Justice Ministry, the judicial branch and the human rights ombudsman are engaged in a subversive movement whose aim is complete power over all branches of government. And they are winning. Despite the efforts of a few officials and magistrates – Valdés, Linares and now President Morales himself – many others have fallen into line.

CONCLUSION
THE RUNAWAY COMMISSION

The CICIG was hired by the UN and Guatemala to do one kind of job, and it has been doing another. This deviation has created a threat to Guatemala as well as to international order. Not only is it being applauded by international "progressives." Quite incongruously, it is being backed politically and financially by the US.

The job that the CICIG pledged to do was to uncover and dismantle extra-legal organizations that impede the practice and enjoyment of popular freedoms. The CICIG commissioner's recent performance at the Wilson Center for International Scholars – which happens to be a US government institution – shows what the CICIG is actually about.

Mr. Velásquez spent his hour talking about what kind of attorney general Guatemala should have. Even more than endorsing a particular candidate for the job, Velásquez asserted the CICIG's right – indeed, its duty – to make a character judgment about Guatemala and its government; and, if necessary, to act on behalf of its view.

This pattern has been in place for a long time. In 2010, an earlier CICIG commissioner effectively demanded the removal of an earlier attorney general, supposedly because that official had unspecified connections to the criminal world. Those charges were never filed; Attorney General Conrado Reyes was removed from office by means of a fraudulent maneuver in which the CICIG played a central role. Far from being in the past, the illicit removal of Reyes is very much in the present day; the current CICIG commissioner attempted to justify it to his Washington audience in March 2018.

Rather than address the endemic problems of Guatemala's security, as it had pledged to do, the CICIG has simply used the country's problems as a pretext for increasing its own prosecutorial and political power. Three years ago, a Guatemalan citizen petitioned the CICIG with a request that it investigate illegal militias that had established their own de facto rule over large areas of western Guatemala. Mr. Velásquez answered this request by writing to the justice minister, saying the CICIG had more important things on its agenda than this kind of investigation.

Mr. Velásquez had it all wrong; that citizen, Karen Ness, was urging the CICIG to do no more or less than fulfill its mission. Ms. Ness, who is also a US citizen, actually traveled to the March 2018 Washington conference to press Mr. Velásquez on the matter. Mr Velásquez evaded and squirmed before giving Ms. Ness the characteristic answer of a bureaucrat: "We receive so many requests to investigate . . ."

An ironic facet of the situation is that the CICIG has been granted freedom from any oversight or discipline. Not even the world's elite political bodies or military forces have been given that kind of autonomy; even they have to answer to some form of authority. Not, however, the CICIG; its diplomatic immunity has enabled it literally to get away with murder. At the same time, the judicial authority in Guatemala has granted that the CICIG may not be sanctioned for diplomatic misbehavior.

When diplomats overstep their bounds, they are subject to expulsion from the country in which they have committed the violations. In August 2017, the president of Guatemala invoked his absolute authority, under constitutional and international law, to declare Mr. Velásquez persona non grata and to insist on his expulsion. An international outcry, led by President Trump's State Department, ensued; and Guatemala's highest court, which now has a pro-CICIG majority, blocked the president's action.

The CICIG refuses to be bound by Guatemala's constitution, by its executive authority, or by international law. It has also directed

CONCLUSION
Guatemala's judicial authorities to support its lawlessness.

To date, the CICIG's enforced predominance has had these effects, among others, on Guatemalan society:
- It has enabled a clique of subversive forces – ex-guerrilla, militias and others – to play a grossly oversized, even a dominant, role in the country's governance;
- It has created an element of terror in society and thus violated the Law of National Reconciliation, which concluded Guatemala's internal armed conflict;
- It has stripped away the sense of certainty that institutions governing by law would otherwise provide;
- Its overtly political agenda has grabbed attention and resources away from efforts to combat ordinary criminality, which has left the ordinary populace feeling quite undefended.

Finally, the CICIG has indicated its next move: just as it aspires to have a "constructive" attorney general in office, so will it act to install a president of like mind. In the CICIG's lexicon, it is the next logical step. In the language of politics, it is called subversion.

This has now become a problem for the United States. As long as its ambassador to Guatemala poses for photos with Mr. Velásquez in back of a sign that says "I {heart} CICIG;" as long as US members of Congress and diplomats pronounce official support for this runaway institution; as long as the US continues to furnish up to 90 per cent of the CICIG's operating budget; and as long as official US institutions like the Wilson Center devote their time and resources to giving Mr. Velásquez a platform, the US has a responsibility to pay attention and make things right.

The CICIG is undermining the fabric of Guatemala's freedom. Its actions have been furthering the very kinds of extra-legal, freedom-threatening entities it was called upon to eradicate. The security of the hemisphere, and the integrity of the US's Southern border, will be on the line if Guatemala's constitutional order collapses. It's time

CRIMES WITHOUT PUNSHIMENT

for the US to honor the sovereignty of Guatemala, to understand the CICIG for what it is, and to get out of the way so that Guatemala's president and Congress can act constitutionally regarding the runaway commission.

AFTERWORD
The Ministry of Virtue
by Armando de la Torre

The CICIG was bound to be corrupt. So would any entity that was born with an exclusive license to practice coercion.

The CICIG, or the International Commission Against Impunity in Guatemala, is the offspring of culturally limited minds and perverse intentions. With its unrestricted license to prosecute in Guatemala, the CICIG has paralyzed our civic life and has sown uncertainty everywhere. Among the results, we have seen a freeze on investments along with burgeoning unemployment.

Adding insult to injury, the CICIG's directors have been foreigners who had never set foot in Guatemala, much less worried about the future of our children and grandchildren. Still worse, they arrived with arrogant prejudices about the country's culture — a product of their own ignorance and that of the international bureaucrats who anointed them.

This was only to be expected. From the moment that the CICIG was publicly proposed in 2005, I deplored it and spoke on behalf of the lawsuit to declare it unconstitutional.

The CICIG is unconstitutional to its roots. Its activities come from a deep-seated, predatory animal nature which cries out for restraint — especially as the actors are foreigners who show contempt for the local populace.

The CICIG staff are endowed with privileges and powers like those of no other public officials on earth. They enjoy lifetime immunity along with their juicy salaries. They are invited to use the testimony of "protected" witnesses — often false — against whomever they wish. They may conduct surveillance without limits. They may, and they do, fabricate evidence.

They have the power — which they have used liberally — to subject others to years of confinement without having to obtain convictions. Perhaps most crucially, they have removed the presumption of innocence from Guatemala's justice system, thereby denying citizens their most basic right to self-defense.

All the while, the CICIG is not accountable to Guatemalan authorities — not even to the public prosecutor's office, as everyone else is. Guatemala's entire judicial system has become a tool of the CICIG, which rules it with a dictator's arbitrariness.

Even as the CICIG staff are endowed with an international platform and unlimited access to Guatemalan media — not to mention broadly favorable coverage in US media — they remain beyond scrutiny. Their behavior is arrogant, ungrateful, arbitrary, and cruel. In the present day they stand alone, but we have met their like before: the Dutch slave traders; the Belgians who colonized the Congo; the Viking raiders who lorded it over the North Sea and the Mediterranean; the Nazi mass murderers who made fortunes in iron and nickel; and those Swiss, unworthy to claim descent from William Tell, who stole the bank deposits of wealthy Jews massacred in Auschwitz and Bergen-Belsen.

This is the panorama in which the CICIG's current commissioner, a Colombian political adventurer by the name of Iván Velásquez, demands to be seen. Velásquez has been proposed as a running mate by Colombian presidential candidate Gustavo Petro, a former commander of the M-19 guerrilla group. This arrangement has actually gained approval from some prominent members of the Guatemalan private sector.

Thanks to those incautious and not-overly-bright citizens, as well

AFTERWORD

as to a handful of European powers which meddle in everything Guatemalan, we have been submerged in a coup d'état at the hands of so-called anti-impunity commissioners who have turned our justice ministry and our highest courts into their very own Ministry of Virtue.

Did the CICIG not arrive here with a pretense of helping with our justice system, before it mounted the corrupt monstrosity that now rules over us?

Guatemala, arise and move yourself!

CRIMES WITHOUT PUNSHIMENT

UN Commission in Guatemala the Enemy of Its Own Mandate

There is a UN entity that has flown under the radar internationally and been misunderstood in Guatemala, where it operates. The lack of awareness needs to change, because the CICIG (its Spanish acronym) is unaudited and not accountable to any jurisdiction on the planet.

The CICIG, created in 2006 with the stated mission of fighting clandestine security organizations, has engaged in a long line of objectionable activity. However, the recent plight of the Bitkovs, a CICIG-persecuted exile Russian family in Guatemala, has caught the attention of the US Commission on Security and Cooperation in Europe, better known as the Helsinki Commission.

The CICIG's activities are now receiving long-awaited scrutiny, particularly because they enjoy US taxpayer funding and State Department political support. However, what it hasn't done is even more telling than what it has done.

On May 18, 2018, a court in San Marcos province in southwest Guatemala and bordering Mexico issued a revealing ruling, as recounted by local radio. In effect the court told the local population that they are under the rule of illegal armed gangs protected by the criminal-justice system and the CICIG. These two institutions turn an ideological blind eye to their Marxist allies.

Yet the funding and support from the State Department continues under the Trump administration—the rule of law and Guatemala's elected government be damned.

In 2014, US reporters visited San Pablo, San Marcos, and discovered its inhabitants were repressed by a criminal structure. One member of the structure was the URNG, the guerrilla umbrella group that became a political party after the 1996 peace accords. The objective of the URNG and associated groups in San Pablo was to stop the construction of a local hydroelectric project, which local residents supported because of the many benefits it offered, including jobs.

San Pablo inhabitants were forced to participate in criminal activities such as blocking roads and police access and occupying and destroying private property. Anyone who resisted faced cut off water and electricity, no access to school for their children, and beatings and kidnappings.
In 2013, these gangs threw a local resident, Casimiro Pérez, into a clandestine prison and threatened him with being burned to death after his wife had attended an event of the hydroelectric project. To avoid that fate, Pérez had to carry large rocks from a river to a road, which took him and his four minor children a week to finish. Pérez filed a complaint with the Justice Ministry.

Two years later, a mob forcibly removed Pérez from his residence, threw him into a hole, and threatened to burn him alive. They then marched him with his arms tied in front of an angry mob to the location of the hydroelectric plant, and the mob destroyed the machinery and the installations. In the confusion, Pérez escaped.

A concerned citizen filed a complaint with the CICIG about Pérez's treatment. Six weeks later, Commissioner Iván Velásquez wrote a letter to the justice minister, copied to the complainant, in which he said the case was not among his priorities. The Justice Ministry took no action.
At the trial for the 2013 Pérez kidnapping, the court acquitted one defendant and convicted another on a lesser charge that carried no

jail time. They did so in an arbitrary manner by accepting Pérez's testimony for one defendant while rejecting the same testimony for the other. The acquitted defendant was a leader of a local gang and the same person who, claiming he was an indigenous authority, had threatened the US reporters.

In its May 18 ruling on Pérez's 2015 kidnapping complaint—for what the mob did to him in the burning of the hydroelectric plant—the court acted in a similar manner. The defendant was convicted of a lesser crime than kidnapping and sentenced to two years in jail, but the penalty is commutable if the convicted person pays about $500.

Besides those who were tried, Pérez had named many other participants in the actions against him in his complaints to the Justice Ministry. None of them have been arrested, and they circulate freely in the area. The ringleader, with an arrest warrant against him, still managed to be elected mayor on the URNG ticket. The police did not bother to arrest him while he was out in public as a candidate.

The message to the communities in the area is that the gangs are in charge, and it stems directly from the CICIG refusing to act on the 2015 complaint.

The CICIG's stated purpose is to protect "the right to life and to personal integrity" of citizens from vigilante groups that "commit illegal acts"—those linked to "agents of the State or [with] the capacity to generate impunity for their illegal actions." The San Pablo events show the CICIG has become exactly what it was created to eliminate. Former US Vice President Joe Biden traveled to Guatemala three times in 12 months and publicly linked US aid to the continuance of the CICIG. US support for the UN commission gives it responsibility for the nefarious suppression of these locals, which also promotes the unfortunate result of an increase in the flow of illegal migrants and drugs to the United States.

The Liga was a co-plaintiff in the case of the 2013 Pérez complaint.

Made in the USA
Columbia, SC
03 July 2023